the
cat owner's
maintenance log

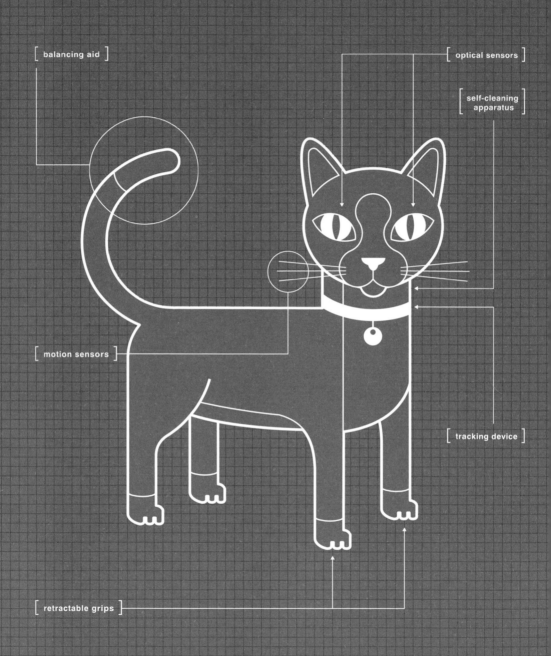

[balancing aid]

[optical sensors]

[self-cleaning apparatus]

[motion sensors]

[tracking device]

[retractable grips]

the
cat
owner's maintenance log

A RECORD OF YOUR FELINE'S PERFORMANCE

by Dr. David Brunner and Sam Stall

Illustrated by Paul Kepple and Jude Buffum

QUIRK BOOKS
PHILADELPHIA

THE CAT OWNER'S MANUAL

ISBN 1-931686-87-4

A veterinarian for 25 years and operator of Indianapolis's Broad Ripple Animal Clinic for 22 years, DR. DAVID BRUNNER specializes in treating small animals—cats and dogs. He has two daughters, Molly and Kendell, two black Labrador retrievers, and a wonderful cat named Mouse. He is also the coauthor of *The Dog Owner's Manual*.

SAM STALL is the coauthor of *The Dog Owner's Manual* and the author of *The Good, the Bad, and the Furry*. He resides in Indianapolis with his three terrier mixed-breeds, Tippy, Katie, and Gracie, as well as his wife, Jami (who has no terrier blood whatsoever), and their cat, Ted.

Copyright © 2005 by Quirk Productions, Inc.

Illustrations copyright © 2005 by Headcase Design

All rights reserved. No part of this book may be reproduced in any form without written permission from the publisher.

ISBN: 1-59474-048-8

Printed in China • Typeset in Swiss

Design and illustrations by Paul Kepple and Jude Buffum @ Headcase Design

Distributed in North America by Chronicle Books • 85 Second Street • San Francisco, CA 94105

10 9 8 7 6 5 4 3 2 1

Quirk Books • 215 Church Street • Philadelphia, PA 19106 • www.quirkbooks.com

Contents

[front]

[left side]

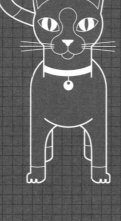

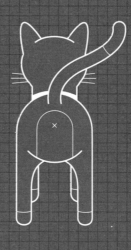

[right side]

[back]

Welcome
to Your New Cat!

Congratulations on the acquisition of your new cat.

This product's value as a companion and source of entertainment is legendary throughout the world. Favored by everyone from ancient Egyptian pharaohs to present-day big-city apartment dwellers, the cat is one of history's most popular, most recognized brands. With proper care and maintenance, it can become a favorite with you, too.

The cat is surprisingly similar to other high-tech devices you may already own. Like personal digital assistants, it is compact and portable. Like a home security system, it is capable of functioning autonomously for extended periods without direct human intervention. And, *unlike* virtually any other product on the market, it is, for the most part, self-cleaning.

With proper guidance, this near-autonomous system can master numerous desirable behaviors. It can even provide companionship and love. All that's required is that you attend to its relatively modest programming, fuel, and maintenance needs. That's where *The Cat Owner's Maintenance Log* can be of assistance. This book is designed to serve as a convenient collection point for data on your model's development, medical issues, and much more. It also contains essential information on various cat-related issues that can help the novice owner solve common feline quandaries.

You'll find annual maintenance checklists for keeping track of the milestones in every year of your feline's service life. At the back of the log you'll also discover various primers on cat behavior, including tips on determining daily fuel requirements, how to calculate its age in "cat years," and national organizations to contact for technical support. A convenient envelope is provided for storing medical records, photographs, and mementos.

Good luck—and enjoy your new cat!

Owner's Record

OWNER INFORMATION

○ ○ ○   First Name   Initial   Last Name
Mr.   Mrs.   Ms.

○ ○ ○   First Name   Initial   Last Name
Mr.   Mrs.   Ms.

Address (Number and Street)   Apt. #

City   State/Province   Zip/Postal Code

MODEL'S BIRTH DATE

☐ ☐ / ☐ ☐ / ☐ ☐ ☐ ☐

Month   Day   Year

MODEL'S ACQUISITION DATE

☐ ☐ / ☐ ☐ / ☐ ☐ ☐ ☐

Month   Day   Year

MODEL'S GENDER

○ ○
Male   Female

MODEL'S NAME

Casual Name   Pedigreed Name (If Any)

MODEL'S DIMENSIONS

Weight   Length   Height

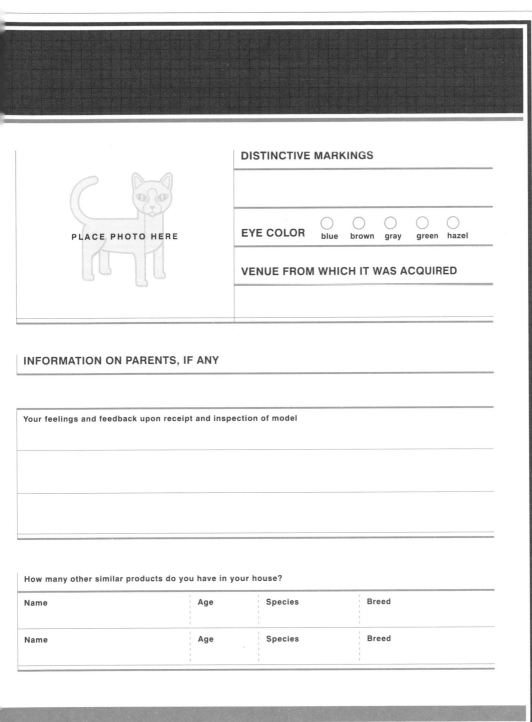

PLACE PHOTO HERE

DISTINCTIVE MARKINGS

EYE COLOR   ○ blue   ○ brown   ○ gray   ○ green   ○ hazel

VENUE FROM WHICH IT WAS ACQUIRED

INFORMATION ON PARENTS, IF ANY

Your feelings and feedback upon receipt and inspection of model

How many other similar products do you have in your house?

Name	Age	Species	Breed
Name	Age	Species	Breed

Breed Specification

CHECK ALL THAT APPLY:

❏ Abyssinian

❏ American Bobtail
❏ American Curl

❏ American Shorthair

❏ American Wirehair

❏ Balinese

❏ Bengal

❏ Birman

❏ Bombay
❏ British Shorthair

❏ Burmese

❏ Chartreux
❏ Colorpoint Shorthair
❏ Cornish Rex

❏ Devon Rex

❏ Egyptian Mau

❏ European Burmese

❏ Exotic Shorthair

❏ Havana Brown

- ❑ Himalayan

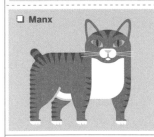

- ❑ Japanese Bobtail
- ❑ Javanese
- ❑ Korat
- ❑ LaPerm

- ❑ Maine Coon

- ❑ Manx

- ❑ Munchkin
- ❑ Norwegian Forest Cat

- ❑ Ocicat

- ❑ Oriental Shorthair

- ❑ Persian

- ❑ Ragamuffin
- ❑ Ragdoll
- ❑ Russian Blue

- ❑ Scottish Fold

- ❑ Selkirk Rex

- ❑ Siamese

- ❑ Snowshoe
- ❑ Somali

- ❑ Sphynx

- ❑ Tonkinese
- ❑ Turkish Angora
- ❑ Turkish Van
- ❑ Other: _____

QUICK REFERENCE GUIDE : If any of these standard parts appea

THE HEAD

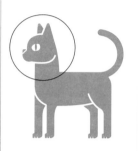

EYES: Each model contains two. Feline irises form a distinctive vertical slit, rather than the circle common in most mammals. The visual system is protected by a "third eyelid" that deploys from the interior corner of each eye socket.

EARS: Each model contains two. A cat's outer ear can rotate 180 degrees, allowing it to scan its environment for particular sounds and pinpoint them with great precision.

NOSE: The cat's sense of smell is superior to that of humans, but markedly inferior to that of dogs. A newborn kitten's nose is already so finely tuned that it can differentiate one of its mother's nipples from the others via smell.

TONGUE: The hundreds of tiny barbs covering its surface are used for several tasks— including scraping meat from the bones of prey; washing and grooming the coat; drying wet fur; and acting as a temperature control system (by relieving overheating through panting). Cats drink by forming a depression in the front of their tongues and using it to convey liquid to their mouths.

TEETH: Felines do not chew their food; they chop it. Adult domestic cats come equipped with 30 teeth, all of which are designed for shredding meat. They use their large fangs, or "canines," to break the necks of their prey. In the case of domestic felines, these teeth are optimally spaced for dispatching mice.

WHISKERS: Positioned in sets of 12 on each side of the muzzle, these thick, deeply set hairs are highly developed sensory organs. Among other things, they can gauge changes in wind direction and detect nearby movements in extreme low-light environments. They also help the cat determine if it can squeeze through a tight space (the whiskers are usually the same span as the feline's body at its widest point, unless the cat is obese or extremely pregnant). During hunting, the cat can push the whiskers forward, to obtain information about the prey with which it is grappling.

THE BODY

COAT: Most cat coats incorporate three hair types: a topcoat composed of "guard hairs," and an undercoat of bristly "awn hairs" and softer "down hairs." Purebred varieties may lack one or more of these. For instance, the Persian has no or very few awn hairs, and the almost entirely coatless Sphynx carries only a small number of down hairs.

TAIL: Used as a mood-signaling device and as a balancing aid while climbing. It may contain anywhere from 14 to 28 vertebrae.

PAWS: Cats walks on the tips of their "fingers." This design feature optimizes them for sprinting, where they can reach speeds of 31 mph (50 km/h). Cats can have a "dominant" forepaw, just as humans have dominant hands. About 40 percent of cats are left-pawed, 20 percent right-pawed, and 40 percent ambidextrous.

CLAWS: Each paw is equipped with a set of claws optimized for climbing, fighting, and grasping prey. They can be retracted when not in use. This design option is exclusive to felines.

GENITALS: Females reach sexual maturity at 7 to 12 months; males at 10 to 14 months. The head of the male cat's penis is covered with spines, which stimulate ovulation in the female during intercourse.

OUTPUT PORT: Products from the cat's waste discharge system are extremely rich in nitrogen—so rich that they can "burn" vegetation just as an overapplication of fertilizer can.

HEIGHT: Unlike domestic dogs, cats are fairly uniform in size. An average domestic cat stands about 12 inches (30 cm) tall at the shoulder.

NIPPLES: Males and females are equipped with a set of docking ports. They are non-functional in males.

WEIGHT: An adult domestic cat usually weighs between 6 and 12 pounds (3–5.5 kg).

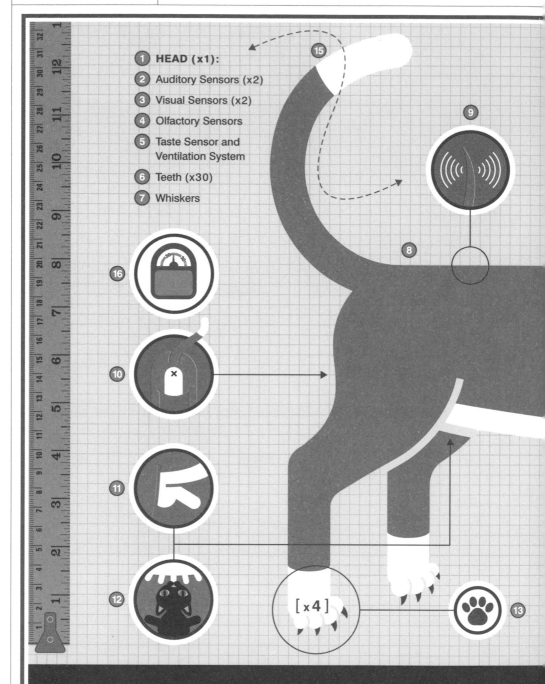

1 **HEAD (x1):**
2 Auditory Sensors (x2)
3 Visual Sensors (x2)
4 Olfactory Sensors
5 Taste Sensor and Ventilation System
6 Teeth (x30)
7 Whiskers

[x4]

STANDARD COMPONENTS LIST: Check your model carefully.

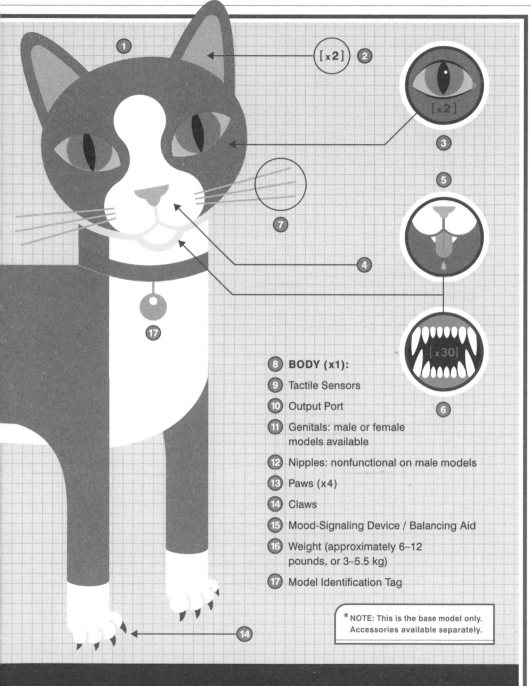

[x2] ②

[x2]

⑧ **BODY (x1):**

⑨ Tactile Sensors

⑩ Output Port

⑪ Genitals: male or female
models available

⑫ Nipples: nonfunctional on male models

⑬ Paws (x4)

⑭ Claws

⑮ Mood-Signaling Device / Balancing Aid

⑯ Weight (approximately 6–12
pounds, or 3–5.5 kg)

⑰ Model Identification Tag

[x30]

> * NOTE: This is the base model only.
> Accessories available separately.

any of the parts shown above are missing, notify your service provider immediately.

SENSOR SPECIFICATIONS

AUDITORY SENSORS: Felines can pick up extremely high-frequency tones—about two octaves higher than those that humans can hear, and half an octave higher than those that dogs can hear. They can triangulate on the location of an individual sound by comparing the minute differences in its tone and arrival time at their two ears. An organ in the inner ear called the vestibular apparatus senses a cat's position in space and allows it to land on its feet (usually) when dropped.

OLFACTORY SENSORS: Felines carry about 19 million scent-receptive nerve endings in their noses, compared to approximately 5 million in humans. They are particularly attuned to nitrogen compounds. Since these compounds are almost always present in food that has begun to rot, the cat's ability to detect them helps it determine if a potential meal is palatable.

VISUAL SENSORS: The cat's vision system is optimized for conditions with minimum lighting. Key hardware modifications include a reflective tissue layer at the back of each eye that increases the amount of light passing through the retinas. This causes feline eyes to "glow" at night. Cats have a wider field of vision than humans (285 degrees versus 210 degrees), but their ability to discern fine detail is only 10 percent that of ours. However, they are exceedingly good at locating, ranging, and attacking moving objects. Contrary to initial beliefs, cats are not color-blind.

TASTE SENSORS: While humans possess some 9,000 taste buds, cats are equipped with fewer than 500. As with humans, cats respond to four broad categories of flavor: sweet, salty, sour, and bitter. Sweet makes the least impression. Because they have difficulty discerning tastes, feline culinary selections are based mostly on odors. This is why foods that smell particularly foul (to humans) can attract them so strongly.

TACTILE SENSORS: Each hair in a cat's coat is connected to a mechanoreceptor nerve that sends environmental information to the brain. Although their stereotypical reputation as "loners" would seem to state otherwise, most cats enjoy being touched. Petting can cause, among other things, a drop in the cat's heart rate and a dramatic decrease in muscle tension. Ironically, it can cause almost the same response in the human doing the petting

NAVIGATIONAL SENSORS: Many scientists assert that cats can sense the earth's gravitational field and use it to find their way, without visual cues, from one distant location to another. This feature may explain the numerous true stories of misplaced cats who travel hundreds of miles over unfamiliar territory to return to their homes.

ADDITIONAL SENSORS: A receptor called Jacobson's organ, which is linked to the roof of the mouth by a duct, detects chemical sexual signals from other felines. Some cats make a lip-curling, snarl-like face in order to bring scents into contact with this sensor.

IMPORTANT CONTACT INFORMATION

PRIMARY VETERINARIAN:

Phone Number ☐☐☐ — ☐☐☐ — ☐☐☐☐ OFFICE / MOBILE

Phone Number ☐☐☐ — ☐☐☐ — ☐☐☐☐ OFFICE / MOBILE

Address

EMERGENCY OR AFTER-HOURS VETERINARIAN:

Phone Number ☐☐☐ — ☐☐☐ — ☐☐☐☐ OFFICE / MOBILE

Address

INSURANCE PROVIDER: Policy Number

Phone Number ☐☐☐ — ☐☐☐ — ☐☐☐☐ OFFICE / MOBILE

Address

GROOMER:

Phone Number ☐☐☐ — ☐☐☐ — ☐☐☐☐ OFFICE / MOBILE

Address

KENNEL:

Phone Number ☐☐☐ — ☐☐☐ — ☐☐☐☐ OFFICE / MOBILE

Address

CATSITTER:

Phone Number [ ][ ][ ] — [ ][ ][ ] — [ ][ ][ ][ ]   OFFICE
MOBILE

Address

ANIMAL SHELTER:

Phone Number [ ][ ][ ] — [ ][ ][ ] — [ ][ ][ ][ ]   OFFICE
MOBILE

Address

Web Site

ANIMAL POISON CONTROL HOTLINE:

Phone Number [ ][ ][ ] — [ ][ ][ ] — [ ][ ][ ][ ]   OFFICE
MOBILE

Address

CONTACT IN YOUR ABSENCE: ◯ Family ◯ Friend ◯ Neighbor

Phone Number [ ][ ][ ] — [ ][ ][ ] — [ ][ ][ ][ ]   OFFICE
MOBILE

Address

OTHER:

Phone Number [ ][ ][ ] — [ ][ ][ ] — [ ][ ][ ][ ]   OFFICE
MOBILE

Address

V I T A L   I N F O R M A T I O N : This data offers a quick, at-a-glance overview

IDENTIFICATION INFORMATION

License Tag Number

Rabies Tag Number

Microchip Identification Number (If Any)

FEEDING

Specific Cat Food Brand

Portion Size

Number of Servings   ◯   ◯   ◯   ◯   ◯
                           1   2   3   4   5

Times of Daily Servings   #1 [ ] : [ ] AM PM   #2 [ ] : [ ] AM PM

#3 [ ] : [ ] AM PM   #4 [ ] : [ ] AM PM   #5 [ ] : [ ] AM PM

Acceptable Snacks

Unacceptable Foods (If Any)

of the status of your model's hardware and software functions.

CHRONIC MEDICAL CONDITIONS

ALLERGIES (IF ANY)

Allergen	Symptoms
Allergen	Symptoms
Allergen	Symptoms

BEHAVIORAL QUIRKS

SUPPLEMENTAL VISUAL DOCUMENTATION

 **Unit's Initial Arrival at New Home:**

 **First Exterior Grooming Session:**

 **Memory Upgrade/Obedience Training:**

Interactions with Family Members:

SUPPLEMENTAL VISUAL DOCUMENTATION

 Holidays:

 Preferred Feline Associate(s):

 **Additional Documentation:**

Medication Record

DATE	NAME	FUNCTION	DOSAGE

Medication Record

DATE	NAME	FUNCTION	DOSAGE

Vaccination Record

DATE	NAME	NOTES

Vaccination Record

DATE	NAME	NOTES

CAUTION

Currently, there is much debate about which immunizations to administer and, most importantly, how often they can be safely given. Your veterinarian can perform a blood test, known as a "titer," to assess your feline's immunity to various infectious diseases (rabies, etc.) and determine whether booster shots are necessary. Consult him or her for recommendations and the latest data.

Barring emergencies, most cats will require a handful of veterinary visits during their first year of life and annual visits thereafter. Listed below is an approximate guideline of when you should expect to have the cat serviced and what you can expect from your veterinarian. Ideally, a kitten's first visit should take place before it goes to your home.

AGE 8–12 WEEKS

- General physical exam
- Check kitten for parasites (intestinal worms, fleas, ear mites)
- Have kitten dewormed
- Test for feline leukemia and feline AIDS
- If seasonally appropriate, begin heartworm preventative

- Discuss which vaccines to administer and when to give them
- If seasonally and environmentally appropriate, begin flea and tick medications
- Discuss any issues of feline maintenance you may have questions about, including grooming, feeding, litter box protocols, etc.

AGE 11–15 WEEKS

- General physical exam
- Have kitten dewormed
- Check kitten for parasites

- Administer veterinarian-recommended vaccinations
- Discuss behavior problems, if any

AGE 14–17 WEEKS

- General physical exam
- Have kitten dewormed
- Check kitten for parasites
- Discuss appropriate time for spaying/neutering; schedule procedure

- Administer veterinarian-recommended vaccinations
- Discuss behavior problems, if any
- Discuss transition to adult-formula cat food
- Discuss changes in heartworm preventative dosage to reflect kitten's increasing size

ANNUALLY

- General physical examination
- Appropriate immunization boosters
- Deworming (if necessary)
- Heartworm blood test

- Wellness testing for mature cats (initiated at six or seven years of age to evaluate kidneys, liver, blood sugar, and other organ functions)
- If cat lives outdoors, feline leukemia and feline AIDS tests

Feline Developmental Stages

BIRTH TO 8 WEEKS

About two-thirds of kittens are born headfirst, and about one-third tail first. They are born blind, deaf, unable to walk, and weighing only about 4 ounces (113 g). Eyelids open at 10 to 12 days of age. Ears open at 14 to 17 days. Kittens begin to crawl at 16 to 20 days, to walk at 22 to 25 days, and to run at 4 to 5 weeks. Consumption of solid food begins at 3 to 4 weeks.

8 TO 15 WEEKS

Full weaning takes place at or before 8 weeks. Kittens can be supplied with small amounts of thinned gruel (dry food mixed with water) as early as their third or fourth week. As time passes, the amount of liquid in the meal can be reduced and the solid matter increased. All baby or "milk" teeth are present at 8 weeks. Males begin to outweigh females at approximately 10 weeks of age. At 12 weeks, eye color (which in very young kittens is almost always blue) changes to permanent adult hue. The first physical exam, stool check, and immunization should occur at 9 weeks. Kittens may leave their mother for a new home anywhere from the age of 8 to 10 weeks, depending on when they make the transition to solid food. This transition should occur automatically, without human input.

15 WEEKS TO ADULTHOOD

Permanent "adult" teeth appear between 12 and 18 weeks. Spaying of females can take place as early as 16 weeks. Males can be neutered as early as 16 weeks. While female cats reach their adult weight at roughly 12 months of age, males keep growing until about 15 months.

Spaying and Neutering

BIRTH TO 8 WEEKS

It is the duty of every responsible pet owner to have his or her feline spayed or neutered. Unwanted litters contribute to a vast oversupply of cats in the world. This is a particular problem because felines, if left unchecked, can reproduce in staggering numbers over a short period.

Unless you plan to breed your cat (which is not recommended, except in the case of highly valued purebred models), it should be sterilized before reaching sexual maturity. For males this is called *neutering* (removal of the testicles); for females, *spaying* (removal of the ovaries and uterus). Without neutering, the habits of a male cat (marking its territory with urine; engaging in fights with other males; patrolling ceaselessly in search of females in heat) can be nearly intolerable. The neutering process deletes these subroutines along with the testicles. Neutered males also experience fewer health problems.

Likewise, female cats spayed before puberty are spared such malfunctions as uterine and ovarian cancer—two common disorders. Female cats will also stop going into heat (a two-week-long trial of house-soiling and howling that occurs two or more times each year).

Financial Records

Use this section to create a financial "snapshot" of costs associated with the care,
your choosing (three months, six months, a year) and then total them. If you find the

VETERINARY VISITS		
Date	Reason for Visit	Cost
		$
		$
		$
		$
		$
		$
		$
		$

VETERINARY PROCEDURES (surgeries, teeth cleanings, etc.)		
Date	Procedure	Cost
		$
		$
		$
		$
		$
		$
		$
		$

PET INSURANCE		
Year Policy Began	Policy Provider	Yearly Premium
		$

maintenance, and comfort of your feline unit. Simply record expenses for the time period of experience valuable, use these pages as a template for a financial record of your own creation.

MEDICATIONS

Date Prescribed	Medication	Cost
		$
		$
		$
		$
		$
		$
		$
		$

FOOD (if necessary, estimate total expenditure)

Date	Variety	Cost
		$
		$
		$
		$
		$
		$
		$
		$
		$
		$
		$
		$

Financial Records

GROOMING

Date	Name of Shop	Cost
		$
		$
		$
		$
		$
		$

KENNEL CARE

Date	Name of Kennel	Duration of Stay	Cost
			$
			$
			$
			$
			$
			$

OBEDIENCE OR OTHER TRAINING

Date	Nature of Training	Cost
		$
		$
		$
		$
		$

ACCESSORIES (toys, bedding, etc.)

Date	Description	Cost
		$
		$
		$
		$
		$
		$
		$
		$

MISCELLANEOUS

Date	Description	Cost
		$
		$
		$
		$
		$
		$
		$
		$
		$
		$
		$
		$

ANNUAL PERFORMANCE EVALUATION

Use the following pages to track the performance and operation of your feline. Be sure to document any visits to your service provider. You might also wish to note important events such as first car trip, the completion of litter box training, any significant malfunctions, and so on.

YEAR 1

DATE ☐☐ / ☐☐ / ☐☐ through ☐☐ / ☐☐ / ☐☐

VACCINATION RECORD

| ☐☐ / ☐☐ | Type | Information |
| Month / Day | | |

| ☐☐ / ☐☐ | Type | Information |
| Month / Day | | |

| ☐☐ / ☐☐ | Type | Information |
| Month / Day | | |

| ☐☐ / ☐☐ | Type | Information |
| Month / Day | | |

MEDICATIONS

| ☐☐ / ☐☐ | Type | Information |
| Month / Day | | |

| ☐☐ / ☐☐ | Type | Information |
| Month / Day | | |

| ☐☐ / ☐☐ | Type | Information |
| Month / Day | | |

MALFUNCTIONS

| ☐☐ / ☐☐ | Type | Information |
| Month / Day | | |

| ☐☐ / ☐☐ | Type | Information |
| Month / Day | | |

| ☐☐ / ☐☐ | Type | Information |
| Month / Day | | |

When selecting a name for a new feline, remember that the most effective ones are short and usually end with a long "ee" sound. Good choices include Dolly, Ally, and Teddy. Try to avoid monikers that contain pronounced hissing sounds (Sissy, Sheba, etc.), and resist the urge to give complicated names, such as Alexandra.

VACCINATION RECORD

☐☐ / ☐☐	Type	Information
Month Day		
☐☐ / ☐☐	Type	Information
Month Day		
☐☐ / ☐☐	Type	Information
Month Day		
☐☐ / ☐☐	Type	Information
Month Day		

MEDICATIONS

☐☐ / ☐☐	Type	Information
Month Day		
☐☐ / ☐☐	Type	Information
Month Day		
☐☐ / ☐☐	Type	Information
Month Day		

MALFUNCTIONS

☐☐ / ☐☐	Type	Information
Month Day		
☐☐ / ☐☐	Type	Information
Month Day		
☐☐ / ☐☐	Type	Information
Month Day		

When training a cat, use food treats to encourage performance. Praise, especially at the beginning of a difficult data download, will usually not be enough to initiate the desired behavior. Later, after the behavior has been mastered, the feline can often be weaned away from the treat reward.

DATE ☐☐ / ☐☐ / ☐☐ through ☐☐ / ☐☐ / ☐☐

VACCINATION RECORD

Month	/ Day	Type	Information
☐☐	☐☐	Type	Information
☐☐	☐☐	Type	Information
☐☐	☐☐	Type	Information
☐☐	☐☐	Type	Information

MEDICATIONS

Month	/ Day	Type	Information
☐☐	☐☐	Type	Information
☐☐	☐☐	Type	Information
☐☐	☐☐	Type	Information

MALFUNCTIONS

Month	/ Day	Type	Information
☐☐	☐☐	Type	Information
☐☐	☐☐	Type	Information
☐☐	☐☐	Type	Information

When playing with a kitten or cat, always direct its playful aggression toward toys. Never allow them to pounce or smack at your hands or other extremities. They may get the message that launching attacks on unsuspecting humans is acceptable behavior.

VACCINATION RECORD

| ☐☐ / ☐☐ | Type | Information |
| Month / Day | | |

| ☐☐ / ☐☐ | Type | Information |
| Month / Day | | |

| ☐☐ / ☐☐ | Type | Information |
| Month / Day | | |

| ☐☐ / ☐☐ | Type | Information |
| Month / Day | | |

MEDICATIONS

| ☐☐ / ☐☐ | Type | Information |
| Month / Day | | |

| ☐☐ / ☐☐ | Type | Information |
| Month / Day | | |

| ☐☐ / ☐☐ | Type | Information |
| Month / Day | | |

MALFUNCTIONS

| ☐☐ / ☐☐ | Type | Information |
| Month / Day | | |

| ☐☐ / ☐☐ | Type | Information |
| Month / Day | | |

| ☐☐ / ☐☐ | Type | Information |
| Month / Day | | |

To dissuade your cat from climbing drapes (a common form of feline amusement), secure the window coverings using spring-tension rods, which will fall on the model if it attempts to climb. Once the cat experiences this, it will, in most cases, discontinue the behavior.

YEAR 5

VACCINATION RECORD

☐☐ / ☐☐
Month   Day

Type

Information

☐☐ / ☐☐
Month   Day

Type

Information

☐☐ / ☐☐
Month   Day

Type

Information

☐☐ / ☐☐
Month   Day

Type

Information

MEDICATIONS

☐☐ / ☐☐
Month   Day

Type

Information

☐☐ / ☐☐
Month   Day

Type

Information

☐☐ / ☐☐
Month   Day

Type

Information

MALFUNCTIONS

☐☐ / ☐☐
Month   Day

Type

Information

☐☐ / ☐☐
Month   Day

Type

Information

☐☐ / ☐☐
Month   Day

Type

Information

If your cat makes a habit of trying to bolt out open doors, the first step is to make sure the feline never succeeds. If it does, the temptation to repeat the behavior will be strongly reinforced. Coach children to be mindful of the cat, and never access an exterior door while your arms are laden with packages. You will be unable to foil an escape attempt.

YEAR 6

VACCINATION RECORD

Month	Day	Type	Information
[ ] [ ]	/ [ ] [ ]		
[ ] [ ]	/ [ ] [ ]		
[ ] [ ]	/ [ ] [ ]		
[ ] [ ]	/ [ ] [ ]		

MEDICATIONS

Month	Day	Type	Information
[ ] [ ]	/ [ ] [ ]		
[ ] [ ]	/ [ ] [ ]		
[ ] [ ]	/ [ ] [ ]		

MALFUNCTIONS

Month	Day	Type	Information
[ ] [ ]	/ [ ] [ ]		
[ ] [ ]	/ [ ] [ ]		
[ ] [ ]	/ [ ] [ ]		

Cats' faces contain scent glands that they use to mark their territory. When a cat rubs its face determinedly against its owner, it is both displaying affection and "marking" that person as its exclusive property.

DATE ☐☐ / ☐☐ / ☐☐ through ☐☐ / ☐☐ / ☐☐

VACCINATION RECORD

| ☐☐ / ☐☐ | Type | Information |
| Month / Day | | |

| ☐☐ / ☐☐ | Type | Information |
| Month / Day | | |

| ☐☐ / ☐☐ | Type | Information |
| Month / Day | | |

| ☐☐ / ☐☐ | Type | Information |
| Month / Day | | |

MEDICATIONS

| ☐☐ / ☐☐ | Type | Information |
| Month / Day | | |

| ☐☐ / ☐☐ | Type | Information |
| Month / Day | | |

| ☐☐ / ☐☐ | Type | Information |
| Month / Day | | |

MALFUNCTIONS

| ☐☐ / ☐☐ | Type | Information |
| Month / Day | | |

| ☐☐ / ☐☐ | Type | Information |
| Month / Day | | |

| ☐☐ / ☐☐ | Type | Information |
| Month / Day | | |

If your cat attempts repeatedly and unsuccessfully to pass a fur ball (and also displays constipation and loss of appetite), the mass may be lodged in the stomach or small intestine. This is a potentially life-threatening malfunction. Consult your veterinarian immediately.

YEAR 8

VACCINATION RECORD

Month	Day	Type	Information
☐☐	☐☐		
☐☐	☐☐		
☐☐	☐☐		
☐☐	☐☐		

MEDICATIONS

Month	Day	Type	Information
☐☐	☐☐		
☐☐	☐☐		
☐☐	☐☐		

MALFUNCTIONS

Month	Day	Type	Information
☐☐	☐☐		
☐☐	☐☐		
☐☐	☐☐		

Some felines can develop allergic reactions to common household items, including the odor of new carpet, freshly painted walls, even the scent of new electronic equipment. Also, a great many cats are allergic to plastic.

YEAR 9

DATE ☐☐ / ☐☐ / ☐☐ through ☐☐ / ☐☐ / ☐☐

VACCINATION RECORD

☐☐ / ☐☐	Type	Information
Month / Day		
☐☐ / ☐☐	Type	Information
Month / Day		
☐☐ / ☐☐	Type	Information
Month / Day		
☐☐ / ☐☐	Type	Information
Month / Day		

MEDICATIONS

☐☐ / ☐☐	Type	Information
Month / Day		
☐☐ / ☐☐	Type	Information
Month / Day		
☐☐ / ☐☐	Type	Information
Month / Day		

MALFUNCTIONS

☐☐ / ☐☐	Type	Information
Month / Day		
☐☐ / ☐☐	Type	Information
Month / Day		
☐☐ / ☐☐	Type	Information
Month / Day		

When cleaning up cat urine, never use an ammonia-based cleaning product. The scent is similar to cat urine and may actually encourage the feline to "visit" the spot again. During cleanup, shine an ultraviolet (black) light on the spot in question. Any remaining deposits of urine will fluoresce, making them easier to detect.

DATE ☐☐ / ☐☐ / ☐☐ through ☐☐ / ☐☐ / ☐☐

VACCINATION RECORD

Month	Day	Type	Information
☐☐	/ ☐☐		
☐☐	/ ☐☐		
☐☐	/ ☐☐		
☐☐	/ ☐☐		

MEDICATIONS

Month	Day	Type	Information
☐☐	/ ☐☐		
☐☐	/ ☐☐		
☐☐	/ ☐☐		

MALFUNCTIONS

Month	Day	Type	Information
☐☐	/ ☐☐		
☐☐	/ ☐☐		
☐☐	/ ☐☐		

In general, felines aged 10 or older are considered to be "seniors." To head off potential age-related problems, it is important to monitor the feline's appearance and behavior and also to schedule regular maintenance inspections with your veterinarian (some recommend twice-a-year visits for older felines).

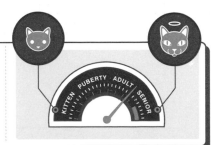

YEAR 11

VACCINATION RECORD

☐☐ / ☐☐	Type	Information
Month / Day		
☐☐ / ☐☐	Type	Information
Month / Day		
☐☐ / ☐☐	Type	Information
Month / Day		
☐☐ / ☐☐	Type	Information
Month / Day		

MEDICATIONS

☐☐ / ☐☐	Type	Information
Month / Day		
☐☐ / ☐☐	Type	Information
Month / Day		
☐☐ / ☐☐	Type	Information
Month / Day		

MALFUNCTIONS

☐☐ / ☐☐	Type	Information
Month / Day		
☐☐ / ☐☐	Type	Information
Month / Day		
☐☐ / ☐☐	Type	Information
Month / Day		

A cat's protein intake is extremely high—about 25 percent of daily calories. Cats do well on high-fat diets, which, among other things, aid them in the absorption of vitamins A and E. The proportion of fat in a cat's diet should increase as it ages.

YEAR **12**

VACCINATION RECORD

☐☐ / ☐☐	Type	Information
Month Day		

☐☐ / ☐☐	Type	Information
Month Day		

☐☐ / ☐☐	Type	Information
Month Day		

☐☐ / ☐☐	Type	Information
Month Day		

MEDICATIONS

☐☐ / ☐☐	Type	Information
Month Day		

☐☐ / ☐☐	Type	Information
Month Day		

☐☐ / ☐☐	Type	Information
Month Day		

MALFUNCTIONS

☐☐ / ☐☐	Type	Information
Month Day		

☐☐ / ☐☐	Type	Information
Month Day		

☐☐ / ☐☐	Type	Information
Month Day		

Grooming is an excellent time to examine your cat for irritated skin, lumps, bumps, ticks, fleas, and any other problem that might require veterinary attention.

DATE ☐☐ / ☐☐ / ☐☐ through ☐☐ / ☐☐ / ☐☐

VACCINATION RECORD

☐☐ / ☐☐	Type	Information
Month Day		

☐☐ / ☐☐	Type	Information
Month Day		

☐☐ / ☐☐	Type	Information
Month Day		

☐☐ / ☐☐	Type	Information
Month Day		

MEDICATIONS

☐☐ / ☐☐	Type	Information
Month Day		

☐☐ / ☐☐	Type	Information
Month Day		

☐☐ / ☐☐	Type	Information
Month Day		

MALFUNCTIONS

☐☐ / ☐☐	Type	Information
Month Day		

☐☐ / ☐☐	Type	Information
Month Day		

☐☐ / ☐☐	Type	Information
Month Day		

Particularly stubborn deposits of cat hair can be removed from rugs, carpets, and upholstery with a damp towel, which bunches up the hair into easily removable balls. Fabric sprays that negate static cling also repel cat hair, as do fabric softener sheets, which can be rubbed over clothing to remove follicular concentrations.

YEAR 14

VACCINATION RECORD

| ☐☐ / ☐☐ | Type | Information |
| Month · Day | | |

| ☐☐ / ☐☐ | Type | Information |
| Month · Day | | |

| ☐☐ / ☐☐ | Type | Information |
| Month · Day | | |

| ☐☐ / ☐☐ | Type | Information |
| Month · Day | | |

MEDICATIONS

| ☐☐ / ☐☐ | Type | Information |
| Month · Day | | |

| ☐☐ / ☐☐ | Type | Information |
| Month · Day | | |

| ☐☐ / ☐☐ | Type | Information |
| Month · Day | | |

MALFUNCTIONS

| ☐☐ / ☐☐ | Type | Information |
| Month · Day | | |

| ☐☐ / ☐☐ | Type | Information |
| Month · Day | | |

| ☐☐ / ☐☐ | Type | Information |
| Month · Day | | |

Ironically, long-haired cats present less-complex shedding problems than short-haired models. While short cat hairs tend to embed in fabric and are difficult to remove, long hairs are easier to spot and pick up.

YEAR 15

VACCINATION RECORD

☐☐ / ☐☐	Type	Information
Month / Day		
☐☐ / ☐☐	Type	Information
Month / Day		
☐☐ / ☐☐	Type	Information
Month / Day		
☐☐ / ☐☐	Type	Information
Month / Day		

MEDICATIONS

☐☐ / ☐☐	Type	Information
Month / Day		
☐☐ / ☐☐	Type	Information
Month / Day		
☐☐ / ☐☐	Type	Information
Month / Day		

MALFUNCTIONS

☐☐ / ☐☐	Type	Information
Month / Day		
☐☐ / ☐☐	Type	Information
Month / Day		
☐☐ / ☐☐	Type	Information
Month / Day		

Keep all medicines away from cats, especially over-the-counter painkillers. Aspirin and ibuprofen are toxic to them, as is the analgesic acetaminophen (the active ingredient in Tylenol).

HAZARD

DATE ☐☐ / ☐☐ / ☐☐ through ☐☐ / ☐☐ / ☐☐

VACCINATION RECORD

| ☐☐ / ☐☐ | Type | Information |
| Month / Day | | |

| ☐☐ / ☐☐ | Type | Information |
| Month / Day | | |

| ☐☐ / ☐☐ | Type | Information |
| Month / Day | | |

| ☐☐ / ☐☐ | Type | Information |
| Month / Day | | |

MEDICATIONS

| ☐☐ / ☐☐ | Type | Information |
| Month / Day | | |

| ☐☐ / ☐☐ | Type | Information |
| Month / Day | | |

| ☐☐ / ☐☐ | Type | Information |
| Month / Day | | |

MALFUNCTIONS

| ☐☐ / ☐☐ | Type | Information |
| Month / Day | | |

| ☐☐ / ☐☐ | Type | Information |
| Month / Day | | |

| ☐☐ / ☐☐ | Type | Information |
| Month / Day | | |

Feeding the cat during family mealtimes may prevent the feline from milling around the table, begging for scraps.

VACCINATION RECORD

☐☐ / ☐☐   **Type**   **Information**
Month   Day

☐☐ / ☐☐   **Type**   **Information**
Month   Day

☐☐ / ☐☐   **Type**   **Information**
Month   Day

☐☐ / ☐☐   **Type**   **Information**
Month   Day

MEDICATIONS

☐☐ / ☐☐   **Type**   **Information**
Month   Day

☐☐ / ☐☐   **Type**   **Information**
Month   Day

☐☐ / ☐☐   **Type**   **Information**
Month   Day

MALFUNCTIONS

☐☐ / ☐☐   **Type**   **Information**
Month   Day

☐☐ / ☐☐   **Type**   **Information**
Month   Day

☐☐ / ☐☐   **Type**   **Information**
Month   Day

If you cannot feel the cat's ribs, the unit may be over-weight. If the ribs are very pronounced, the feline could be underweight. Be advised that the gain or loss of a half pound in a week is reason for a veterinary consultation.

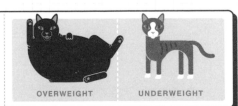

OVERWEIGHT   UNDERWEIGHT

DATE [ ] / [ ] / [ ] through [ ] / [ ] / [ ]

VACCINATION RECORD

Month / Day	Type	Information
[ ] / [ ]	Type	Information
[ ] / [ ]	Type	Information
[ ] / [ ]	Type	Information
[ ] / [ ]	Type	Information

MEDICATIONS

Month / Day	Type	Information
[ ] / [ ]	Type	Information
[ ] / [ ]	Type	Information
[ ] / [ ]	Type	Information

MALFUNCTIONS

Month / Day	Type	Information
[ ] / [ ]	Type	Information
[ ] / [ ]	Type	Information
[ ] / [ ]	Type	Information

Ideally there should be one litter box on every level of your home, or one more than the total number of cats you possess.

$$(\text{🐱} \times n) + 1 = \text{🗑}$$

DATE ☐☐ / ☐☐ / ☐☐ through ☐☐ / ☐☐ / ☐☐

VACCINATION RECORD

| ☐☐ / ☐☐ | Type | Information |
| Month / Day | | |

| ☐☐ / ☐☐ | Type | Information |
| Month / Day | | |

| ☐☐ / ☐☐ | Type | Information |
| Month / Day | | |

| ☐☐ / ☐☐ | Type | Information |
| Month / Day | | |

MEDICATIONS

| ☐☐ / ☐☐ | Type | Information |
| Month / Day | | |

| ☐☐ / ☐☐ | Type | Information |
| Month / Day | | |

| ☐☐ / ☐☐ | Type | Information |
| Month / Day | | |

MALFUNCTIONS

| ☐☐ / ☐☐ | Type | Information |
| Month / Day | | |

| ☐☐ / ☐☐ | Type | Information |
| Month / Day | | |

| ☐☐ / ☐☐ | Type | Information |
| Month / Day | | |

Be sure to secure string, twine, ribbons, dental floss, and other such objects. A cat may ingest these involuntarily due to the design of its tongue, which is lined with inward-pointing barbs, on which string can snag and then work its way down the throat. A feline in such a situation may swallow a considerable amount of material against its will.

YEAR 20

VACCINATION RECORD

☐☐ / ☐☐	Type	Information
Month Day		

☐☐ / ☐☐	Type	Information
Month Day		

☐☐ / ☐☐	Type	Information
Month Day		

☐☐ / ☐☐	Type	Information
Month Day		

MEDICATIONS

☐☐ / ☐☐	Type	Information
Month Day		

☐☐ / ☐☐	Type	Information
Month Day		

☐☐ / ☐☐	Type	Information
Month Day		

MALFUNCTIONS

☐☐ / ☐☐	Type	Information
Month Day		

☐☐ / ☐☐	Type	Information
Month Day		

☐☐ / ☐☐	Type	Information
Month Day		

Aging cats can suffer both from muscle loss and arthritis. To ease strain during feeding time, offer food and water in elevated bowls.

NOTES AND OBSERVATIONS

NOTES AND OBSERVATIONS

[Appendices]

SLEEP MODE

The typical feline sleeps approximately 16 hours a day, which means it spends about 60 percent of its life off-line. The cat's formerly predatory lifestyle necessitated this configuration. Their preferred prey (mice) is most active at dusk and dawn, leaving the daylight hours and most of the night as downtime to be passed in slumber. But instead of taking their rest in one stretch, felines take a number of "catnaps." Even in deepest slumber, a cat is still alert to its environment. The ears of a sleeping cat may twitch in response to sounds, and the slightest movement will instantly awaken it. If the disturbance proves benign, the feline can just as instantly shut down again.

This preference for early evening and early morning activity can cause problems for owners—especially if the cat stays up half the night prowling the house or goes into a frenzy of activity at 5 A.M. The best solution is to engage the cat in strenuous play during daylight hours. The extra exertion will help it (and its owner) sleep through the night.

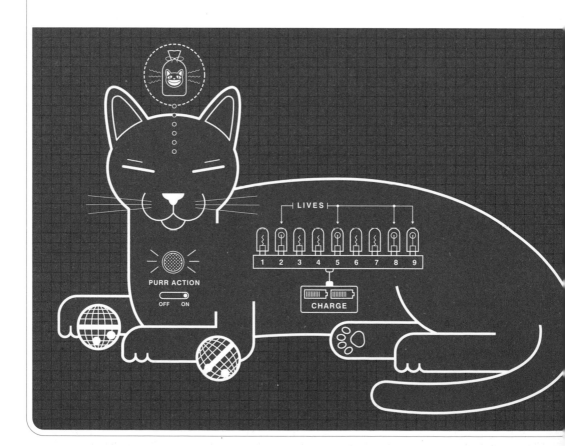

LIVES

1 2 3 4 5 6 7 8 9

PURR ACTION
OFF   ON

CHARGE

PURRING

Do not be concerned if you periodically hear a low-decibel hum emanating from your unit. This is not a malfunction, but a way for your feline to communicate everything from contentment to distress. Experts are not sure how the sound is produced. One theory suggests that the purr originates from a large vein that passes through the diaphragm. The feline may cause it to vibrate via muscle contractions, producing the distinctive sound.

Purring is most useful for mothers and newborn kittens. A mother may purr to let her initially blind and deaf offspring know where she is, and kittens purr (they begin at one week of age) to assure their mother that all is well. Cats purr while interfacing with humans to indicate their contentment or, sometimes, to ask for help. For instance, injured and/or sick cats may purr long and loudly, perhaps as a plea for assistance.

CATNIP

Many cats enjoy interacting with catnip-stuffed toys. Catnip (*Nepeta cataria*) is a member of the mint family. This common herb, also called "catmint," affects felines in much the same way that marijuana does humans. An exposed cat will spend about 10 minutes rolling on and rubbing against the source of the catnip, obviously in great pleasure. Then the interlude ends with the cat (according to the latest scientific studies) suffering no short-term or long-term ill effects. All feline models, including lions, are susceptible to catnip (the herbs valerian and Canadian honeysuckle produce similar reactions). However, not all individual units are affected. Only 50 to 60 percent of adult cats react to catnip, and kittens younger than 2 months are indifferent to it.

DECLAWING

Because the cat's off-the-shelf design is so elegant, owners have rarely been tempted to make postnatal changes. One exception is for the procedure known as declawing, or onychectomy. Usually done to prevent destructive scratching of home furnishings, the operation removes the claws on the forepaws using a technique comparable to the removal of human fingertips at the top knuckle. The procedure can sometimes cause severe, lasting pain for adult cats. Though common in the United States, the modification is against the law in Germany, England, and Switzerland, where it is considered animal cruelty. This procedure should only be contemplated if other methods of stopping excessive clawing (regular nail clipping, behavior modification, and/or placing "caps" on the claws) have failed, and the choice is between performing the procedure or surrendering the cat to a shelter.

TYPES OF FUEL: There are two broad categories of fuel: dry and canned.

DRY FUEL (front view)

APPROXIMATE DAILY FUEL REQUIREMENTS: The typical adult feline requires a daily nutrient total of 1 ounce of canned food or 1/3 ounce of dry food per pound of body weight. (If your cat's operating system is metric-based, provide approximately 60 grams of canned food or 20 grams of dry food for every kilogram of body weight.) Recommended portions are also listed on the containers of prepackaged foods. Be ready to adjust these, however, if the cat becomes overweight or underweight.

Examine the nutritional purpose and ingredients carefully before selecting a brand.

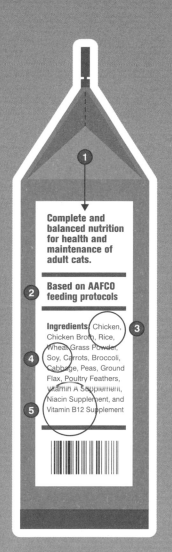

DRY FUEL (side view)

CANNED FUEL (front view)

CANNED FUEL (back view)

1. Nutritional purpose and adequacy statement
2. Indicates a high-quality product that was subjected to a feeding study.

   The order in which the ingredients are listed is determined by weight (heaviest is listed first)

3. Meat should be near the top of the list
4. Cereals and soy should be listed prominently
5. Vitamins, minerals, and preservatives should appear last, as they are used minutely

Calculating Age in Cat Years

A popular misconception is that cats age seven years for each calendar year. In fact, feline aging is much more rapid during the first two years of life. A cat reaches the approximate human age of 15 during its first year, then 24 at age 2. Each year thereafter, it ages approximately four cat years for every calendar year. Thus, a 5-year-old feline would be approximately 36 in cat years. It should be remembered that a cat that lives outdoors ages far more quickly, perhaps even twice as fast, as an indoor cat.

Technical Support

The following organizations offer valuable information and/or services to cat owners.

Animal Poison Control Center (888) 426-4435

Run by the American Society for the Prevention of Cruelty to Animals (ASPCA), the Animal Poison Control Center is staffed 24 hours a day, 7 days a week by veterinarians. They can advise during poison emergencies, provide treatment protocols, and even consult with clients' personal veterinarians. There may be a charge for the service, depending on the circumstances, so have your credit card ready.

American Animal Hospital Association
Member Service Center
(800) 883-6301
www.healthypet.com
Can provide information on AAHA-approved veterinary hospitals in your area.

AKC Companion Animal Recovery
(800) 252-7894
E-mail contact: found@akc.org
A 24-hour hotline to which owners of pets with microchip identification can report their lost animals and/or receive information about their whereabouts.

American Society for the Prevention of Cruelty to Animals
(212) 876-7700
www.apsca.org
Founded in 1866, the ASPCA is the oldest humane organization in the Western Hemisphere. Among many other things, it provides humane education, advice on obtaining medical services, and support for animal shelters.

American Veterinary Medical Association
(847) 925-8070
www.avma.org
A not-for-profit association of roughly 70,000 veterinarians that can provide information on AVMA-accredited facilities in your area.

The Cat Fancier's Association
(732) 528-9797
www.cfainc.org
The world's largest organization for pedigreed cats, the CFA offers data on breeds and primers on feline maintenance. They also sponsor numerous cat shows.

Humane Society of the United States
(202) 452-1100
www.hsus.org
Animal advocacy and information clearinghouse covering such topics as pet adoption, care, and rights.

National Pesticide Information Center
(800) 858-7378
www.npic.orst.edu
Offers free information about the ·toxicity of common compounds such as lawn care and gardening products.

Petswelcome.com
Extensive Internet site offering comprehensive information on traveling with pets, including listings of hotels that allow them; kennels; amusement park pet facilities; and how to cope with emergencies on the road.

Creating a Repair Kit

Most feline-related medical issues should be handled by a veterinarian. However, minor problems can be dealt with at home—and some major problems can be stabilized before transport to a veterinarian's office—using the following equipment. Place all of these items in one container (a small, plastic toolbox is ideal) and position it someplace easily accessible. Include the name and phone number of your veterinarian, along with the phone number of the nearest animal emergency clinic.

The first-aid kit should contain:

❏ Roll cotton and cotton balls

❏ Eyewash

❏ Ice pack

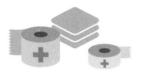
❏ Gauze pads, gauze tape, and surgical tape

❏ Oral syringes

❏ 3-percent hydrogen peroxide

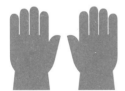
❏ Heavy gloves

❏ Large towels

❏ Thermometer (digital only)

❏ Scissors

❏ Exam gloves

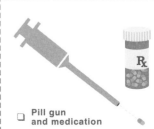
❏ Pill gun and medication